City Shapes

Squares

By Jennifer S. Burke

Children's Press
A Division of Grolier Publishing
New York / London / Hong Kong / Sydney
Danbury, Connecticut

Photo Credits: Cover, p. 11, 13, 15, 17, 19, 21 © Indexstock; p. 5, 7, 9, 21 © Corbis
Contributing Editors: Mark Beyer and Eliza Berkowitz
Book Design: Michael DeLisio

Visit Children's Press on the Internet at:
http://publishing.grolier.com

Library of Congress Cataloging-in-Publication Data

Burke, Jennifer S.
    Squares / by Jennifer S. Burke.
      p. cm. — (City shapes)
    Includes bibliographical references and index.
    Summary: Simple text and photographs reveal different squares that can be found in the city.
    ISBN 0-516-23078-6 (lib. bdg.) — ISBN 0-516-23003-4 (pbk.)
    1. Square—Juvenile literature. [1. Square.] I. Title. II. Series.

  QA482.B89 2000
  516'.15—dc21
                                                                    024038

Contents

There are square shapes all around us!

Some squares are used to play a game.

These black and white squares are used to play **chess.**

There are many tall **buildings** in a city.

Some buildings have square windows.

Try to count how many squares you see.

7

This train has square windows.

Square shapes quickly go by as the train moves.

Can you find any other squares?

9

Some squares are painted on the ground.

You can count the squares as you jump.

How many squares can you count?

11

Signs tell you where to go.

This sign tells you where the **subway** is.

What letter is on this square sign?

Wall Street
Subway Station

② ③ Token booth open:
Mon-Fri 7am to 10:30pm
Other times use
entrance at Wall St

13

There are many different shapes in this picture.

Some square shapes are made when the sun is out.

Which squares are made by **shadows**?

15

This building has square shapes on it.

The square shapes go all around the building.

What color are these squares?

This playground has squares that are for climbing.

How many squares can you find in your playground?

Squares can be on the ground or way up high.

Squares can be black, white, or another color.

Squares in the city are everywhere.

21

New Words

buildings (**bil**-dingz) places where people live or work

chess (**chess**) a board game

shadows (**shah**-dohz) caused when something blocks light

signs (**synz**) things that tell you where to go

subway (**sub**-way) a train that runs below ground

To Find Out More

Books

Circles and Squares Everywhere!
by Max Grover
Harcourt Brace & Company

Silly Squares
by Sophie Fatus
Abbeville Press

Squares and Cubes
by Sally Morgan
Raintree Steck-Vaugn Publishers

Index

About the Author
Jennifer S. Burke is a teacher and a writer living in New York City. She holds a master's degree in reading education from Queens College, New York.

Reading Consultants
Kris Flynn, Coordinator, Small School District Literacy, The San Diego County Office of Education

Shelly Forys, Certified Reading Recovery Specialist, W.J. Zahnow Elementary School, Waterloo, IL

Peggy McNamara, Professor, Bank Street College of Education, Reading and Literacy Program